Taking Steps Towards
Tolerance and Compassion

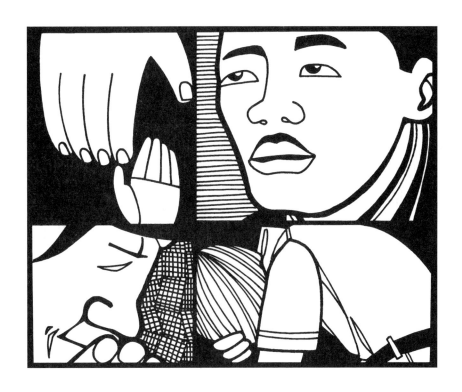

Written by
Linda Schwartz

The Learning Works

The Learning Works

Editor: Kimberley Clark
Illustrator: Bev Armstrong
Cover Photo: Digital Imagery © 2001 PhotoDisc, Inc.
Designer: Kimberley Clark
Cover Designer: Barbara Peterson
Art Director: Tom Cochrane
Project Director: Linda Schwartz

Special thanks to Sue Perona for her feedback and comments.

This book is dedicated to Bev Armstrong—a person who exemplifies kindness, tolerance, and compassion.

Contents

Profiles: People of Tolerance and Compassion • 15–32

Discussion, Drama, and Role-Playing Topics • 33–44

Research and Writing Projects • 45–56

Contents
(continued)

Art Projects • 57–66

Steps to Take Towards Tolerance and Compassion • 67–77

A Note to Kids

When was the last time you asked your mom or dad how her or his day went? How did you recently settle a disagreement with a friend or reach a compromise with a classmate? Have you made time this week to help another person—a senior citizen, a brother or sister, a neighbor, or a friend? Can you name three things you've done recently that show you are a tolerant person?

Your life is probably very busy with school, friends, family, and after-school activities. Sometimes you get so caught up with your own hectic schedule that you don't always take time to step back and think about how you treat other people—those close to you as well as those you don't know very well. Learning how to treat other people with patience, kindness, and open-mindedness is an essential skill. Not everybody you meet is going to share your beliefs and viewpoints. In order to get along at home, at school, at work, and in life, you need to accept differences and treat others with respect, understanding, and tolerance.

Taking Steps Towards Tolerance and Compassion is packed with research, writing, and art projects. There are also discussion, drama, and role-playing topics as well as biographical sketches of men and women of tolerance and compassion.

The ideas presented in this activity book are small steps. None of them alone is enough to change the world. But if you make an effort to incorporate just a few of these suggestions into your life each and every day, the world will be a kinder place in which to live.

tol–er–ance (n)
patience; open-mindedness;
recognition of and respect for the opinions, beliefs, or actions of others

com–pas–sion (n)
the deep feeling of sharing the suffering of another

A Note to Teachers

With today's emphasis on test scores and accountability, many teachers spend a good portion of the school day teaching basics such as reading, social studies, science, and math. However, an equally important responsibility is teaching students how to become caring citizens. But teaching kids how to be tolerant and compassionate is not an easy job.

That is why *Taking Steps Towards Tolerance and Compassion* was written. The pages within this book are packed with creative, easy-to-use activities that you can implement in your classroom. The activities correlate to the curriculum, so you'll find ideas for reading, research, creative writing, poetry, art, and role-playing. Your students will learn about prejudices and about tolerance at home, at school, and in social situations. They'll learn about conflicts and how to resolve them. They'll read biographical sketches of famous men and women of tolerance and compassion. From designing a photo essay to painting tiles for tolerance; from role-playing a disagreement between friends to participating in an empathy exercise about senior citizens—you and your students will enjoy the wide variety of activities the book offers.

One of the special features of the book is compassion tokens that your students pick each week. On the tokens are suggestions for actions students can take to show tolerance and compassion for classmates, for members of their families, for people in the community, and even for themselves. New tokens are selected each week, so it makes for an ideal year-round tolerance program. You can even involve other teachers at your grade level, or make it a school-wide program.

By teaching your students about tolerance and compassion and by encouraging them to take steps to make a difference, no matter how small, you can help them make a difference.

Warm-Ups

What's Your View?

Here are some things to think about, discuss with your classmates, or write about. (Write your responses on a separate piece of paper.)

How would you define tolerance?
Why is it important to be tolerant of others?

Think of an experience you have had
in which tolerance was demonstrated.
How did you feel about it?

In what ways are people throughout the
world alike or similar? What basic needs
do all people have? In what ways
are people different?

Do you think tolerance of other people
is something you are born with or
a value that must be learned through
education and experience?

Taking Steps Towards Tolerance and Compassion
© The Learning Works, Inc.

Warm-Ups
(continued)

How would you define compassion?
Why is it important to be compassionate
towards others?

Tell about a time someone showed
compassion for you or for someone
in your family.

What does the word *conscience* mean
to you? Do you think every person has
a conscience? Explain your answer.

How do you think your conscience helps
you make decisions when it comes
to tolerance and compassion?

Taking Steps Towards Tolerance and Compassion

To the Teacher:

Reproduce the tokens on pages 10-13, using bright-colored paper. Cut the tokens apart, and place all 32 tokens in a decorated box.

Each Monday, ask students to pick one of the tokens in the box. Students have one week to fulfill the assignment on the tokens they selected.

On the following Monday, make time for students to share their experiences and the reactions they got from the recipients of their kind deeds. Each student then selects another token for the week. Acknowledge students who successfully complete their task by giving them a tennis shoe pattern that lists their name and achievement. (See page 14.) Set a class goal of having shoes going all around your classroom denoting the positive steps your students have taken towards tolerance and compassion.

To the Student:

Tolerance and compassion tokens are ideas for simple steps you can take to be kinder to other people throughout the year. Some of the ideas relate to things you can do for classmates and people at school. Others are suggestions for steps you can take at home or out in public. Some are even nice things you do for yourself.

Each Monday, your teacher will let you choose a token. Each token contains an idea for something you can do to show tolerance and compassion. You will have until the following Monday to complete each assignment and will have an opportunity to share your experience with your classmates.

None of these ideas is enough to change the world, but they are small, simple steps you can take to begin to make a difference. These actions will make the people you help feel better and will make you feel better about yourself.

Each time you complete one of the assignments, you will be given an award in the shape of a tennis shoe to fill out and display in the classroom. The goal is to have shoes going all around the room denoting the positive steps you have taken towards tolerance and compassion.

Frequently Asked Questions:

Q What happens if I pick the same token more than once?

A Don't worry! Just do the task for a different person or, in the case of a family member, just repeat the act of kindness. He or she will love it!

Q What if my token says to help someone who is out of school because of illness, and that week no one in my class is absent? Or, what if my token says to do something for my dad and he doesn't live with us?

A Any time a token doesn't apply to your situation, feel free to pick your own act of kindness to do for someone else. Be creative. You might even come up with some ideas that you can add to the token box for classmates to try!

Tolerance and Compassion Tokens

Think of three compassionate people you know. Write a sentence or two describing each of them.

Offer to read a book or play a game with a brother or sister or a neighbor's child.

 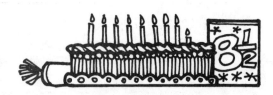

Make up a game you can play to amuse yourself while waiting—in a long line, for an appointment, or while waiting for a friend to join you.

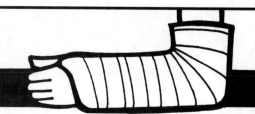

Find a classmate at school who is on crutches or whose arm is in a cast, and offer to help in some way.

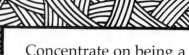

Learn about a unique family tradition one of your classmates observes, such as celebrating a half-year birthday.

Concentrate on being a tolerant, patient listener as people talk. Really hear what they are saying. Wait until they finish speaking before jumping in with your ideas.

Don't lose your cool! Instead of blowing up when you are angry, take some time out to calm down and think about the situation that has upset you. Then choose the best way to deal with the situation.

FREEBIE!
Here's your chance to come up with your own idea for expressing tolerance or compassion to the person of your choice.

Tolerance and Compassion Tokens

Offer to study or review for a test with a classmate who needs help.

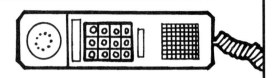

Call a classmate who is absent from school and let him or her know what was covered in class, what assignments were given, and what tests are coming up.

Thank a teacher, a classroom aide, a playground supervisor, a school crossing guard, or another person at school for the good job he or she does.

Say something nice to a classmate with whom you usually don't get along.

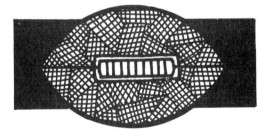

Ask someone who is alone at recess to come and join your game.

Learn three interesting facts about someone in your class whom you don't know very well.

Give up your place at the front of the lunch line to someone who is at the very end of the line. Let the person behind you know what you're doing so he or she saves your place for the other person.

Do something nice for your brother, sister, or another family member when you get home from school today.

Taking Steps Towards Tolerance and Compassion
© The Learning Works, Inc.

Tolerance and Compassion Tokens

Tutor a classmate who needs help in a subject you know a lot about.

Offer to help a neighbor with a chore or an errand. Be sure to get your mom or dad's permission first.

Talk to a classmate who comes from a culture that is different from your own. Learn three interesting facts about his or her culture—a holiday that is celebrated, a food that is eaten, or a special custom that is observed.

Surprise someone at home by doing a chore without being asked.

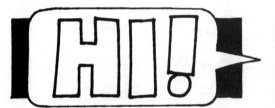

Say hello to someone at school whom you don't know. Look them in the eye and smile.

At home tonight, pay your mom or dad a compliment.

Invite someone sitting alone to join you and your friends at lunch.

Be the first one to say you're sorry the next time you have a disagreement with a friend or family member.

Tolerance and Compassion Tokens

While playing a game at recess, compliment a classmate on a good play or for good sportsmanship.

Let your brother or sister choose what television shows to watch for a whole day.

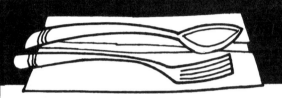

Give special thanks to a waiter or waitress, or to a store clerk. Let him or her know how much you appreciate his or her help.

Tell your mom or dad "I love you" with a big hug, smile, or high five.

While you are in a restaurant or at a store, hold the door open for the person behind you as you enter or exit. Tell the person to have a nice day (or evening).

Pick a classmate you don't know very well. Spend time talking to him or her to learn about this person's family, pets, hobbies, interests, or goals.

Talk things over and make up with someone with whom you haven't been getting along. Make plans to do something together.

Make breakfast in bed or a special snack for someone in your family. (Don't use the oven or stove unless you have your mom or dad's permission.)

Taking Steps Towards Tolerance and Compassion
© The Learning Works, Inc.

Shoe Pattern

To the Teacher

- Reproduce the tennis shoe pattern below.

- At the end of each week, give a shoe pattern to each student in your class who has completed his or her token task.

- Students should fill in their names and a brief description of their achievement on the shoe.

- Ask students to color their shoes with felt-tipped markers or colored pencils. They can also decorate their tennis shoes by adding glitter, sequins, and other embellishments.

- The tennis shoes can then be cut out and displayed on a Tolerance and Compassion bulletin board in your classroom. You can also use the completed tennis shoes to form a border around your room.

Pattern

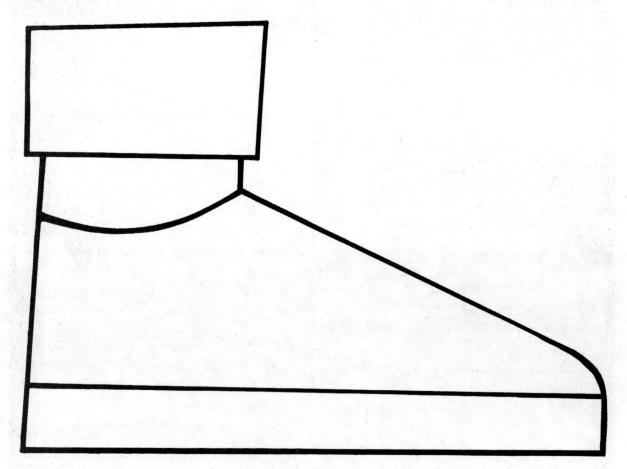

Profiles:
People of Tolerance
and Compassion

Martin Luther King, Jr.

Martin Luther King, Jr., worked for racial equality in the United States and devoted his life to the civil rights movement. He was born in 1929 in Atlanta, Georgia. His father was a minister at Ebenezer Baptist Church, and his mother was a teacher.

Young Martin was an excellent student. He enjoyed reading books, singing, riding his bicycle, and playing football and baseball. When he was very young, he noticed that some people did not treat others with respect. He and other African-Americans could not drink out of the same drinking fountains or use the same public restrooms as white people. African-Americans were kept out of white schools, parks, theaters, hotels, and eating places. They had to sit in separate sections in trains and buses. He listened when his father talked about his hatred of the South's segregation laws. Martin's father felt that all Americans should have the right to use all public places, to earn a living, to vote, and to get a good education. He was a fighter and a role model for his son.

King entered Morehouse College when he was only 15 years old. He made the decision to go into the ministry like his father and grandfather. After his graduation, he entered a school of religion in Pennsylvania, where he studied the world's greatest leaders and thinkers. King was searching for a way to help his people in the struggle against segregation and poverty. He read an essay by Henry David Thoreau, an American writer living more than 100 years ago who believed that a man had the right to disobey any law he thought was evil or unjust. He also studied Mahatma Gandhi, the great leader of India, who taught that people had the right to disobey unjust laws, but in a nonviolent way. King studied the teachings of Jesus Christ, who told his followers to "turn the other cheek" if someone struck them. King gradually refined his philosophy of peaceful, nonviolent protest against unfair laws during these early years at college.

Over the next few years, King graduated at the top of his class, married Coretta Scott, and, in 1954, became minister of Dexter Avenue Baptist Church in Montgomery, Alabama. He worked with the members of his church to help young people go to college. He also worked to help African-Americans register and vote. He saw his church grow day by day. In 1955, King earned his doctoral degree from Boston University.

Martin Luther King, Jr.

(continued)

Then, on December 1, 1955, something happened in Montgomery that changed King's life. An African-American woman, Rosa Parks, refused to give up her seat to a white person. She was breaking the law and was arrested on the spot. The next day, King and other African-American leaders agreed to call a one-day boycott of the buses as a protest. King wasn't sure the boycott would work, but the next day African-Americans were walking, taking cabs, and driving, but none were riding the buses. The bus boycott that was supposed to last one day lasted more than a year. During the days of the boycott, King was arrested, his house was bombed, and he was subjected to personal abuse, but he emerged as a major leader of the civil rights movement. As a result, the Supreme Court declared segregation on buses unconstitutional.

Between 1957 and 1968, Martin Luther King traveled all over the country, appearing wherever there was injustice. He was arrested many times. One time, in 1963, he was arrested for leading a nonviolent demonstration against segregation laws in Birmingham, Alabama. From his prison cell, he wrote the now famous "Letter from a Birmingham Jail," which became an important piece of literature in the civil rights movement. In August 1963, Martin Luther King led a peaceful march on Washington, D.C. More than 200,000 civil rights supporters listened to his moving "I Have a Dream" speech.

In 1965, Dr. King led a march from Selma to Montgomery, the capital of Alabama, to peacefully demonstrate the struggle for voting rights of African-Americans. The first march ended with the marchers being brutally beaten by law enforcement officers. Finally, on March 21, 1965, about 3,200 marchers set out for Montgomery, walking many miles a day and sleeping in fields. Four days later, there were 25,000 marchers. Less than five months after this march, President Lyndon Johnson signed the Voting Rights Act of 1965, enacting legislation that would guarantee voting rights for all Americans.

Martin Luther King received several hundred awards for his leadership in the civil rights movement. He was named Man of the Year by *Time* magazine in 1963, and, in 1964, he received the Nobel Peace Prize, the youngest man to receive the award. He turned over the prize money to the cause of the civil rights movement.

On the evening of April 4, 1968, in Memphis, Tennessee, Dr. Martin Luther King, Jr., was assassinated by James Earl Ray. Dr. King was in Memphis leading sanitation workers in a protest against low wages and intolerable working conditions. The movements and marches that King led brought significant changes to the civil rights movement. He gave African-Americans and poor people a new sense of worth and dignity. In 1986, Martin Luther King, Jr., Day was declared a national holiday in the United States.

"I Have a Dream" Speech

Martin Luther King, Jr. delivered his "I Have a Dream" speech on the steps of the Lincoln Memorial in Washington, D.C., on August 28, 1963. More than 200,000 people attended a demonstration called the March on Washington to commemorate the hundredth anniversary of the Emancipation Proclamation, to call attention to the wrongs suffered by African-Americans, and to try to bring about changes in our society. Here are parts of King's "I Have a Dream" speech.

Five score years ago, a great American, in whose symbolic shadow we stand, signed the Emancipation Proclamation. This momentous decree came as a great beacon light of hope to millions of Negro slaves, who had been seared in the flames of withering injustice. It came as a joyous daybreak to end the long night of captivity.

But one hundred years later, we must face the tragic fact that the Negro is still not free. One hundred years later, the life of the Negro is still sadly crippled by the manacles of segregation and the chains of discrimination. One hundred years later, the Negro lives on a lonely island of poverty in the midst of a vast ocean of material prosperity. One hundred years later, the Negro is still languishing in the corners of American society and finds himself an exile in his own land. So we have come here today to dramatize an appalling condition.

I say to you today, my friends, that in spite of the difficulties and frustrations of the moment, I still have a dream. It is a dream deeply rooted in the American dream.

I have a dream that one day this nation will rise up and live out the true meaning of its creed: "We hold these truths to be self-evident: that all men are created equal."

I have a dream that one day on the red hills of Georgia the sons of former slaves and the sons of former slave owners will be able to sit down together at a table of brotherhood.

I have a dream that one day even the state of Mississippi, a desert state, sweltering with the heat of injustice and oppression, will be transformed into an oasis of freedom and justice.

I have a dream that my four children will one day live in a nation where they will not be judged by the color of their skin, but by the content of their character.

I have a dream today.

— *Dr. Martin Luther King, Jr.*

"I Have a Dream"
(continued)

Activities

- Find the "I Have a Dream" speech on the Internet and read it in its entirety.

- Enhance your vocabulary by finding the meaning of the following words taken from this speech:
  - momentous
  - decree
  - withering
  - captivity
  - prosperity
  - languishing
  - exile
  - appalling

- Illustrate any four of the words listed above.

- Write a paragraph expressing your thoughts on the parts of Martin Luther King's dream that you think have been fulfilled.

- Write a paragraph expressing your thoughts on the parts of his speech that you feel have not yet been accomplished.

- Write a short story or poem related to tolerance and peace in the world. Your poem does not have to rhyme.

- Divide a sheet of white art paper into two sections as shown. Draw a picture from the "I Have a Dream" speech in the first box. Then, in the second box, draw yourself in a picture of an event that is connected to the first picture.

Mother Teresa

Agnes Gonxha Bojaxhiu grew up in Skopje, Albania (now Macedonia). She was a good student and liked to read books and play the mandolin. But what she really looked forward to was going to the Catholic church to pray and sing. Her parents taught her to care for the poor and needy, and the family never turned away anyone who came to their home for help. Young Agnes grew up to become one of the world's greatest and most honored humanitarians—known to everyone around the world as Mother Teresa.

When Agnes was 12 years old, she became very interested in Catholic missions. She wanted to become a missionary nun in India. She learned about the Sisters of Our Lady of Loreto who were active in India, and, in 1928, she went to the order's headquarters in Ireland. There she learned English and was trained in religious life. She chose Sister Teresa as her name.

Soon Sister Teresa was on her way to India. Her religious training continued in Darjeeling, a town at the foot of the Himalayas, and in Calcutta, where she helped care for starving and helpless mothers. In Calcutta, she taught geography and history in a girls' high school. In 1937, Sister Teresa took her final vows in the Loreto order. She was appointed the mother superior of the high school, and Sister Teresa became Mother Teresa.

In 1948, Mother Teresa was granted permission to start a new order of nuns in India. She called the new order the Missionaries of Charity. She rented a room for a school in a slum where there were many neglected and abandoned children. She didn't have any furniture, blackboards, or chalk, but she was able to teach the children to read and to keep clean. Supporting herself by begging, she began another small school and opened a small medical clinic to care for the poor. She also established orphanages to provide homes for children who did not have parents to care for them.

> People who love each other fully and truly are the happiest people in the world. They may have little, they may have nothing, but they are happy people. Everything depends on how we love one another.
>
> — *Mother Teresa*

Mother Teresa
(continued)

As other women joined the order, Mother Teresa was able to expand her charitable projects. She oversaw humanitarian causes in more than 30 countries. She was responsible for establishing a number of medical centers to treat specific diseases, including a leper colony in West Bengal and a hospice for patients with AIDS in New York City. In 1982, she persuaded the Israelis and Palestinians to stop shooting long enough to rescue a group of children from a hospital in besieged Beirut. She is also credited with motivating thousands of people to follow her example and become involved in a variety of humanitarian causes.

Mother Teresa received many awards for her work, including the Pope John XXIII Peace Prize, the Jawaharlal Nehru Award for International Understanding, and the Nobel Peace Prize. In 1985, President Ronald Reagan presented her with the American Presidential Medal of Freedom.

On September 5, 1997, Mother Teresa died in the Mother House of the Missionaries of Charity in Calcutta. She had given herself totally and unconditionally to the service of the poor and needy.

Mother Teresa
(continued)

Activities

1. A *humanitarian* is a person who acts unselfishly for the benefit of others and is committed to improving their lives. Work with your classmates to make a list of humanitarians of the past and present. Explain why you think humanitarian service is important.

2. Read other articles or a book about Mother Teresa. What qualities did she have that made her a unique person? In your opinion, what was her greatest humanitarian contribution? Compare your answer with the answers of others in your class.

3. Even though one person can make a difference, sometimes it is easier to work together with others to reach important goals. Find out about charitable organizations in your area. With the help of your teacher or another adult, learn more about the organizations. Find out if there are ways you and your classmates can help. Report your findings to your class.

4. Choose one of these famous quotations by Mother Teresa and design a card, create a work of art, or write a poem to express your interpretation of the meaning of the quotation.

   • "Little things are indeed little, but to be faithful in little things is a great thing."

   • "We can do no great things; only small things with great love."

   • "If we worry too much about ourselves, we won't have time for others."

   • "I am grateful to receive [the Nobel Peace Prize] in the name of the hungry, the naked, the homeless, of the crippled, of the blind, of the lepers, of all those people who feel unwanted, unloved, uncared-for throughout society, people that have become a burden to the society and are shunned by everyone."

5. Learn more about the Nobel Peace Prize and the recipients of this award. If you were to choose one person to receive this award, whom would you choose and why?

Mahatma Gandhi

Mohandas Karamchand Gandhi was popularly called *Mahatma*, which means "Great Soul." Gandhi was born in 1869 in Gujarat, India. When he was 13, his parents arranged his marriage to another 13-year-old, Kasturbai Makanji.

After studying law in London, Gandhi moved to South Africa and worked as a lawyer. One day, he was forcefully evicted from a first-class train compartment. This incident opened his eyes to the racial discrimination and humiliation faced by nonwhites. He began to develop a unique creed of resistance against injustice, which he called *satyagraha*. Followers of *satyagraha* were encouraged to have compassion for suffering, to spread literacy, and to work to remove social inequalities. *Satyagraha* included doing acts of penance, organizing strikes, and defying certain laws. Gandhi was frequently jailed as a result of the protests he led. Gandhi stayed in South Africa for 21 years. Before he returned to India with his wife and children, he had radically changed the lives of Indians living in South Africa.

Gandhi began leading the Indian struggle for independence from Britain. He realized that some educated Indians were committed to working for independence, but the rest of the people weren't involved in the struggle. They were poor, illiterate, and divided by language and religious differences. Gandhi felt he had to express his ideas to these people in ways they would understand. He decided to wear the Indian loincloth to symbolize poverty. This became his standard dress from that time forward. Gandhi also lived a simple life. He observed that while machines made the lives of some people easier, they also put thousands of laborers out of work. He advocated hand spinning and weaving to produce a homemade cloth called *khadi*.

Mahatma Gandhi
(continued)

Gandhi never wavered in his belief in nonviolent protest and religious tolerance. Sometimes, when Muslim and Hindu citizens committed acts of violence against the British who ruled India or against each other, Gandhi would fast until the fighting stopped. He was arrested many times by the British, but his efforts brought about important reforms.

In 1930, Gandhi led hundreds of followers on a 240-mile march to the sea, where they made salt from sea water. This was a protest against the Salt Acts, which made it a crime to possess salt that was not purchased from the British. During World War II, Gandhi continued his struggle for India's freedom through nonviolent disobedience to British rule. He was jailed for the last time in 1942.

Independence from Britain came in 1947, but to Gandhi's despair, the country was partitioned into Hindu India and Muslim Pakistan, and riots broke out. The last two months of Gandhi's life were spent fasting in an attempt to end the violence, an act which finally stopped the riots.

In January of 1948, on the eve of independence, Gandhi was assassinated by a Hindu fanatic who feared Gandhi's program of tolerance for all religions. Gandhi's righthand man, Jawaharlal Nehru, became India's first prime minister.

Mahatma Gandhi's belief in nonviolence inspired people around the world—from the civil rights and peace movements of North America to the campaign against apartheid in South Africa. As Gandhi said: "There is no path to peace. Peace is the path."

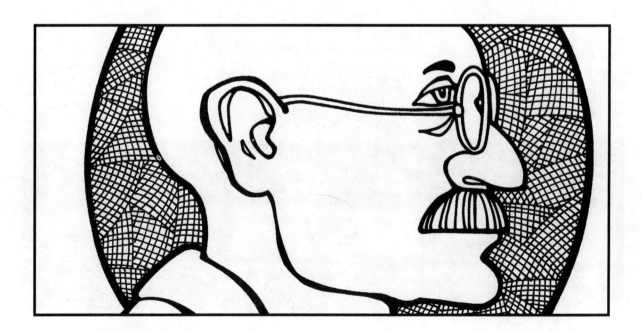

Mahatma Gandhi

(continued)

Activities

1. Think about ways people protest against intolerance or injustice. Make a list of some of the advantages and disadvantages of each form of protest. Here are some examples to get you thinking:

   - boycotts

   - sit-ins

   - marches

   - riots

   - letter-writing campaigns

   - letters-to-the-editor

2. Pretend you are a famous television interviewer who can travel back in time to interview Mahatma Gandhi. Make up three thought-provoking questions you would ask him.

3. Tell whether you agree or disagree with the following statements. Explain your answers.

   - The best way to overcome injustice is to follow the idea of nonviolence.

   - Nonviolent ways of working for justice are too slow.

   - People should disobey laws that they want to see changed.

4. In his struggles for equality in Africa, Nelson Mandela used some of Mahatma Gandhi's nonviolent tactics, such as boycotts, nonviolent protests, strikes, and civil disobedience. Learn more about Nelson Mandela and his contributions towards equality in Africa. Present your research in the form of a poster, a biography, or a newspaper story.

5. Gandhi showed that he identified himself with the poor people of India by wearing a simple, hand-woven loincloth like the ones they wore. Do you have an item of clothing that identifies you as being part of a certain group, such as a team T-shirt, hat, or jacket?

Muhammad Yunus

Muhammad Yunus was an idealistic professor when he started teaching economics in the small Asian country of Bangladesh. He was excited about introducing his students to the many new economic theories he learned as a Ph.D. student at Vanderbilt University in the United States. He knew that his native Bangladesh was one of the world's poorest and least developed nations. He saw many poor people in the villages surrounding the university, but he didn't understand poverty. How could people who worked twelve hours a day, seven days a week, lack sufficient food to feed themselves?

Yunus decided to leave the classroom and go into the villages to learn about poverty. At first he thought that the poor lacked skills or were lazy, but he soon realized that they possessed extraordinary survival skills.

He took a survey of 42 villagers and found out that they each needed only $26.00 to start their own businesses. He loaned them the money they needed and required only that they promise to repay the loan. That was the beginning of the Grameen Bank. (*Grameen* means rural in Bengali.) His bank was unusual because it provided credit to people who were too poor to qualify for traditional bank loans.

Some of his loans went to people who were buying cows, raising chickens, planting home gardens, or grinding grain. Other loans allowed people to start small businesses. At village meetings, bank representatives shared information about proper nutrition and good sanitation, production methods, and marketing techniques.

In 1995, Yunus started Grameen Telecom, a company that established cellular telephone service in rural areas. Loans were made to people to buy phones, and then these people sold the telephone service to their neighbors. He also started a company called CyberKiosks, or village computer centers. These centers made it possible for Grameen borrowers to access the Internet to search for information on jobs, education, agriculture, and marketing. Young people trained in CyberKiosk became resources for teaching others, even those in remote villages.

Today, more than 2.3 million Bangladeshis from more than 38,000 villages have borrowed from Grameen Bank, and there are Grameen programs replicated in 58 countries on 4 continents. Muhammad Yunus has received many awards for his humanitarian work with the poor, including his nation's highest award, the Bangladeshi Independence Day Award.

Muhammad Yunus

(continued)

Activities

1. Evaluate the projects that Muhammad Yunus accomplished and choose the one that impresses you the most. Create a new humanitarian award that you will present to Yunus. Write a short presentation speech that explains the award and the reasons Yunus was chosen to be honored.

2. Pretend that you are going to be given a loan to start a small business from your home. Work with a classmate and select a business such as a lawn service, a dog-walking business, a window-washing service, a company that designs greeting cards and banners on the computer, or any other business. Write a business plan that includes:

   • a description of the business

   • a list of all the tools, equipment, furnishings, materials, and supplies you will need

   • the amount of money you will need to get started

   • a description of how the money from the loan will be spent

   List and divide the responsibilities involved in opening the business you have chosen.

3. Write a newspaper editorial that supports Muhammad Yunus's economic theory of lending money to the needy to help them support themselves and their families.

4. Muhammad Yunus lives with his family in Dhaka, Bangladesh. Find out more about Bangladesh—its size, population, government, climate, natural resources, literacy rate, and average annual income. Present your findings in the form of a written report or poster.

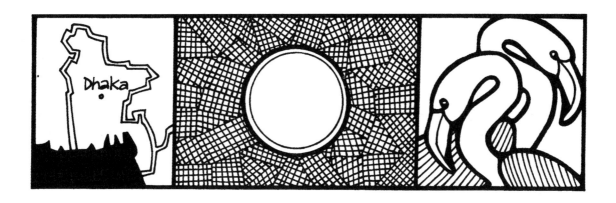

César Chávez

César Chávez, best known for founding and leading the first successful farm workers' union in the United States, was born in 1927 on a small farm near Yuma, Arizona. During the Great Depression, César's family lost their farm. His family and thousands of other displaced families migrated throughout the Southwest, laboring in fields and vineyards. Young César left school after the eighth grade and continued farm work to help support his family. These early experiences taught him that farm laborers encountered many hardships, especially poor labor conditions, racial discrimination, exposure to pesticides, poor sanitation conditions, and low salaries.

As he grew up, Chávez lived by a philosophy dedicated to nonviolence, public action, solidarity, and respect for all cultures, religions, and lifestyles. He practiced the nonviolent methods of Martin Luther King, Jr., and Mahatma Gandhi.

One of Chávez's dreams was to create an organization to help farmers. He led nonviolent strikes and boycotts and went on personal hunger strikes to make people aware of the conditions that farm laborers had to endure. One successful strike-boycott lasted five years and rallied millions of supporters to the cause. He brought together unions, church groups, students, minorities, and consumers. The first collective bargaining agreement between farm workers and growers in the United States was signed in 1966. It required that all farm workers have rest periods, clean drinking water, hand-washing facilities, and clothing that protected them against pesticides.

Another large-scale organized walkout took place in California's Coachella Valley during the summer grape harvest in 1992. The farm workers protested a lack of drinking water and sanitary facilities. They won concessions from the growers. Also in 1992, in the San Joaquin Valley, Chávez organized walkouts and protests. In the Salinas Valley, Chávez led more than 10,000 farm workers on a protest march in support of better conditions in the fields.

Chávez and his union were successful in raising the wages of farm workers and improving their work conditions. In 1991, Chávez received the Aguila de Oro, Mexico's highest award, presented to people of Mexican heritage who have made major contributions outside of Mexico. In 1994, a year after his death, Chávez was presented the Presidential Medal of Freedom, the highest civilian honor in the United States. This was presented posthumously by President Bill Clinton to Chávez's wife, Helen, and their children.

César Chávez
(continued)

Activities

1. How did César Chávez fight on behalf of farm workers? What rights did he think were important? Use the information you learned to create a poster, poem, or collage that highlights Chávez's fight for farm workers.

2. Several times, César Chávez went on a hunger strike to protest conditions of farm workers. Write a persuasive letter to Chávez during one of his hunger strikes. Offer at least three reasons why he should stay on the strike, or why he should give up the strike.

3. Learn the definitions of these words, and use each one in a sentence that demonstrates that you understand its meaning:

   - strike
   - nonviolence
   - walkout
   - posthumously
   - boycott
   - collective bargaining
   - depression
   - union
   - hunger strike

4. Learn about what life is like as a young farm laborer. Read more about migrant farm workers, and then write a journal entry that describes the life of a young migrant farm worker.

Further Study

1. Learn more about the men whom César Chávez admired: Mahatma Gandhi, Martin Luther King, Jr., and St. Francis of Assisi. Write a short story about each one of them. Compare and contrast their causes, their methods of protest, and the outcomes of their humanitarian efforts.

2. Make a timeline of the life of César Chávez. Include some important historical events that took place during his lifetime.

Taking Steps Towards Tolerance and Compassion
© The Learning Works, Inc.

Anne Frank

Anne Frank was born in 1929. Four years later, Adolf Hitler succeeded in becoming chancellor of Germany. Almost immediately, he and his Nazi forces began to arrest political opponents, Jews, Gypsies, and others whom he regarded as inferior. Anne's family was Jewish, and although her father, Otto Frank, had a successful business in Frankfurt, Germany, he realized he should move his family to a safer location. In 1933, the family emigrated to Amsterdam, the Netherlands. Anne attended a nearby Montessori school, made many friends, and excelled in her studies.

For several years, the Frank family lived peacefully in the Netherlands, but then the Nazis invaded the country and conquered it. The occupation meant years of repression, slave labor, hunger, and fear. Under Nazi law, Anne was forced to leave the Montessori school and attend the Jewish Secondary School. In February of 1941, the Nazis began arresting the Netherlands' Jews and sending them to concentration camps and gas chambers.

Anne's father had already planned to go into hiding to save his family. Thanks to the help of several of his employees, he managed to find a place to hide. They began to convert the house where his company was located into a hiding place. The house was like many others in the old part of Amsterdam. It actually consisted of two houses built one behind the other—one in front, a courtyard in the middle, and then an annex. The hideout consisted of the two upper floors and attic of the annex. The entrance to the hiding place was hidden behind a hinged bookcase. The windows at the back were blackened out and painted over, hiding the annex from view.

When Margot, Anne's older sister, received a notice from the Nazis to report for work detail at a labor camp, Otto realized the time had come to go into hiding. On July 6, 1942, the family moved to the secret annex. Moving in with them were Hermann van Pels, Otto's business partner; Auguste, his wife; and Peter, their sixteen-year-old son. Later that year, Fritz Pfeffer, a dentist, joined the group.

Many people in Amsterdam knew that what the Nazis were doing was morally wrong. Several of these people helped the Frank family. They provided food bought on the black market or with food stamps obtained by the underground. By helping to hide the Frank family, they were participating in one of the most dangerous ways of resisting and defying the Nazis. To hide Jews was considered a terrible crime by the Nazis, yet almost every day that the Franks spent in hiding, these people brought food and supplies to the secret annex.

Anne Frank
(continued)

On her thirteenth birthday, in 1942, Anne received a diary from her parents. She immediately began writing in it and continued for the two years that she was confined in the annex. She wrote about her perceptions of the life that she led, describing the times when she was miserable and also the times when she experienced happiness and joy in the midst of hardship and suffering.

Anne knew the danger she and her family were in. In one diary entry she wrote,

> Evening after evening the green and gray army lorries trundle past. The Germans ring at every front door to inquire if there are Jews living in the house. If there are, then the whole family has to go at once. If they don't find any, they go on to the next house. No one has a chance of evading them unless one goes into hiding.

She also recognized the risk that many kind people took. Anne wrote,

> There is a great number of organizations, such as the Free Netherlands, which forge identity cards, supply money to people underground, find hiding places for people, and work for young men in hiding, and it is amazing how much noble, unselfish work these people are doing, risking their own lives to help and save others.

On August 4, 1944, their hiding place was betrayed by a Dutch collaborator. Anne and the others were deported to Westerbork camp. A few weeks later, the inhabitants of the camp were moved to Auschwitz and later to other camps. As starvation, cold, and disease swept through the camps, Margot developed typhus and died. A few days later, Anne died of the same disease. She was 15 years old.

Otto Frank was the only annex inhabitant who survived World War II. When he returned to Amsterdam after the war, he was given Anne's notebooks and papers, which had been retrieved from the annex. Among these papers was her diary, which Otto Frank published in 1947.

Anne Frank
(continued)

Activities

1. Anne wrote in her diary about the unselfish work that some people were doing in Amsterdam, risking their own lives to help and save others. She would probably consider these people heroes. Heroes don't always have to risk their lives to be heroic. For example, a person can be a hero for standing up for someone who is being mistreated, showing kindness to a sick or unhappy friend, or speaking up when something seems morally wrong. Make a list of things you could do that would be heroic. Discuss ways that children your age can do humanitarian or heroic deeds involving risk and/or sacrifice in your home, school, or community.

2. Learn more about the following vocabulary words; then use them in a short paragraph that describes something about Anne Frank's life.

    Nazi   occupation   humanitarian   collaborator   deported   typhus

3. Anne wrote in her diary nearly every day. Pretend that you are Anne's friend and know about the secret hiding place. You have a diary too. Write two entries that describe your feelings about Anne being confined, about the courage of the people helping her, and the reasons why you are keeping the hiding place a secret.

4. Anne wrote this in her diary:

    > People will always follow a good example; be the one to set a good example, then it won't be long before the others follow. . . . How lovely to think that no one need wait a moment, we can start now, start slowly changing the world! How lovely that everyone, great and small, can make their contribution toward introducing justice straightaway. . . . And you can always, always give something, even if it is only kindness!

    Show that you understand the meaning of this entry by drawing a picture, making a poster, or writing a poem or short essay about the theme of this diary entry.

5. Write a paragraph describing what kind of person you think Anne would have become if she had survived the concentration camps. What career would she have chosen? What would have been her favorite activities? Would she have been involved in humanitarian causes? Which ones?

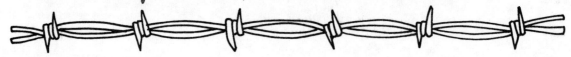

Discussion, Drama, and Role-Playing Topics

PURIM

Odwira

Kwanzaa

TET

Black History Month

URINI NAL

World Understanding and Peace Day

Ramadan

Cinco de Mayo

Thanksgiving Day

What Is Prejudice?

To be prejudiced about someone or something is to form an opinion based on false or incomplete information. We may "pre-judge" people before getting to know them. Sometimes we pre-judge foods we haven't tasted, places we haven't visited, games we've never played.

- We may express our prejudices by being outwardly hostile or simply avoiding people or things we don't like.

- A prejudice may be directed towards an individual person, or towards all the members of a group such as a race or religion.

- Often, prejudiced opinions are based on stereotypes—beliefs that people who share one characteristic are also alike in other ways, for example, "People from that country are lazy and dirty," or "Rich people are stuck up and selfish."

Classroom Discussion Topics

- Have you ever been a victim of prejudice? If so, explain.

- Discuss some of the stereotypes people have about each of these groups of people:

  - teenagers
  - elderly people
  - blonds
  - motorcycle riders
  - homeless people

Role-Playing Idea

- Role-play a situation in which three senior citizens are sitting on a city bench as a group of motorcycle riders with tattoos and leather jackets rides into town.

What Is a Conflict?

In order to be a tolerant person, you must be able to resolve conflicts. A conflict is the tension or struggle caused by opposing needs, ideas, wishes, or demands.

Here are some examples of conflicts:

- teenagers and parents trying to agree on curfews

- a community deciding whether to build a library or a sports arena

- deciding whether to visit your grandmother on her birthday or play in your soccer semifinal, which is scheduled on the same day

When confronted with a conflict, here are some suggestions and steps you can take:

- Identify your choices.

- Evaluate these choices by considering the advantages and disadvantages of each.

- Consider the consequences of these choices. With each, what will you gain and what will you give up?

- Select the choice you know is right, the one that offers the most advantages and the fewest disadvantages, or the one likely to produce fewer un-pleasant consequences.

- Learn from your mistakes. If you resolve a conflict by making a choice you later regret, use this experience to help you make a better and wiser choice next time.

Classroom Discussion Topics

- Describe a conflict in your family that is not too personal. It could be a conflict over a curfew, or the way someone dresses. Describe how a compromise was reached to resolve this conflict.

- What conflicts can arise in your community between neighbors? Give examples of conflicts and describe how they might be resolved.

- Name a conflict that is going on in the world today. What steps are being taken to resolve this problem?

Role-Playing Ideas

- Role-play a situation where a student moves to a new city. His or her hairstyle and clothes are very different from those of the kids at the new school.

Taking Steps Towards Tolerance and Compassion
© The Learning Works, Inc.

Resolving Conflicts Between Friends

When you and a friend have a conflict, following these steps may help you resolve it:

- Determine what the disagreement is really about.

- Decide what you want and what you are willing to give up.

- Acknowledge what your friend wants and ask what he or she is willing to give up.

- Negotiate a compromise that allows each of you to have some of what you want.

- As you negotiate, maintain your own integrity. Set limits and know where you stand. Don't give in or give up on the things that are really important to you. Ask for what you need, but also be willing to give up something as well.

Classroom Discussion Topics

- Describe a conflict you had with a friend. What was the disagreement about? How did each of you compromise to settle the conflict?

- What are some of the ways you can become a better listener?

- Describe a time a friend or classmate showed you special compassion, kindness, or tolerance. What were the circumstances of the incident? How did you feel?

Role-Playing Ideas

- Role-play a situation in which two friends are having a disagreement. Show how they resolve their conflict through compromise and discussion rather than by getting angry or physically fighting.

- Role-play a situation where three friends are out together and two of them exclude the third. Show how the third friend feels and how the conflict is resolved.

- Role-play a situation where you have to tell your best friend you can't come to his or her birthday party because of a family commitment. Show how you could resolve this conflict.

Tolerance at Home

Living together as a family is not always easy. When people with different personalities and viewpoints live together, there are bound to be times when not everyone agrees or gets along. When disagreements arise at home, showing a little tolerance will go a long way.

Here are some steps you can take to resolve differences at home:

- Try being more patient and understanding. Try to see the situation from the other person's point of view.

- Try to reach a compromise in which each person sacrifices something to reach an agreement.

- When there are disagreements in your family, take time to talk about how you feel.

- If you are upset during a disagreement, tell the other person you need time to calm down. Then talk about the problem after things have settled down.

Classroom Discussion Topics

- Does your family have special rules for dealing with conflicts at home? If so, describe them.

- What are some constructive ways you let off steam when you are upset about things that happen at home?

- Give an example of a time you were patient and forgiving with a family member who had hurt or bothered you.

Role-Playing Ideas

- Role-play a disagreement between you and your parent(s) about a curfew you feel is unfair. Remember that in some situations parents "get more votes" because of their position of responsibility and authority.

- Role-play a situation in which your younger brother or sister refuses to give you any privacy and is constantly coming into your bedroom and getting into your things without your permission.

- Role-play a situation where family members all compromise to reach an agreement over an important issue.

- Role-play an argument among four family members who all want to go to different places for a one-week vacation.

- Role-play a situation where an older sibling monopolizes the telephone to the point that none of your friends can get through to you.

New at School

Sizing Up the Situation

Your family has just moved to a new community. Leaving your close friends behind and starting all over at a new school has been tough on you.

This is your first week at school, and although you've tried to talk to the other kids, you haven't really connected with anyone. For the last few days you've eaten lunch alone in the cafeteria. It makes you feel left out and lonely to see all the other kids sitting, talking, laughing, and eating in groups all around you.

Classroom Discussion Topics

- Is it the teacher's responsibility to make sure that new students are made to feel part of the class?

- Have you ever moved to a new neighborhood and started all over in a different school? If so, describe how you felt the first week. What helped you the most in adjusting to the new situation?

- If a new student came to your class, what could you do to make him or her feel welcome?

- Tell about a time you went out of your way to make someone feel welcome.

Role-Playing Ideas

- Role-play a situation in which a new classmate asks to join your circle of friends at lunch.

- Role-play a situation showing how you could make a new student feel welcome during the school day.

- Role-play a time you felt left out and lonely.

Religious Observance

Sizing Up the Situation

Imagine that you belong to a minority religious group. One of the your religion's most sacred holidays will fall on a Monday, and you plan to miss school to observe the holiday with your family. The problem is that a final exam in social studies is planned for Tuesday, and your teacher has announced that on Monday she will be reviewing the material that will be covered on the final. You would really benefit from the review, but you will have to miss it because of the observance of your holiday.

Classroom Discussion Topics

- Is the teacher showing a lack of tolerance towards your religion by planning a major review on the day of your holiday?

- Should you ask your teacher to change the date of the review even though only you are affected?

- Some teachers may have students from five or six minority religious groups in their class. How can students become more understanding and tolerant of the difficulties teachers face in these situations?

Role-Playing Ideas

- Role-play a situation in which someone at school is being teased because of his or her religious beliefs. Show how the incident is resolved.

- Role-play a situation in which a student explains his or her religious customs and holidays to classmates.

Taking Steps Towards Tolerance and Compassion
© The Learning Works, Inc.

Sticking Up for a Friend

Sizing Up the Situation

While at a party, you hear a group of kids saying unkind things about one of your best friends who isn't there. The things the kids are saying about your friend are not true.

Classroom Discussion Topics

- Would you come to a best friend's defense if people were talking about him or her behind his or her back?

- Why do you think kids spread rumors about other people?

- Describe a time when kids said things about you that weren't true. How did you feel?

- Tell about a time a friend came to your defense against a group of kids who were spreading rumors about you.

- Describe a time you stuck up for a friend when he or she wasn't there.

- Have you ever been in a group situation where you said unkind things about another person? How did you feel?

Role-Playing Ideas

- Role-play a situation in which you stick up for a friend against a group of kids who are teasing or picking on her or him.

- Role-play a situation in which you and your friends are at a party. Another person joins your group and begins telling you something about a classmate you know is not true. Show how you would handle the situation and tell this person not to spread rumors.

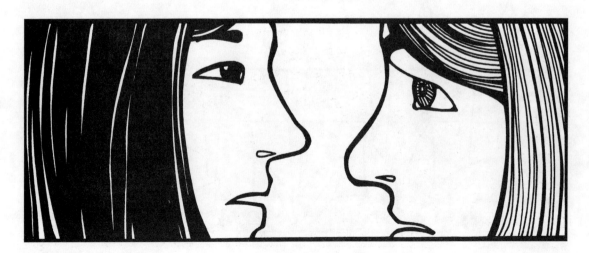

Being Teased

Sizing Up the Situation

Someone at school is constantly teasing you. You've tried to be tolerant and patient, but the teasing is really getting to you.

Classroom Discussion Topics

- If talking to the person who is always teasing you doesn't work, to whom can you turn for help at school? At home?

- Why do you think some kids pick on and tease others? How does it make the kids doing the teasing feel?

- Describe a time someone was constantly teasing you. Were you able to get them to stop? If so, how?

- If you're with a group of kids who start to tease someone, should you get involved and try to stop them?

- Have you ever tried to stop a kid who was teasing someone? What did you do? What happened? Would you try to confront someone again?

Role-Playing Ideas

- Role-play a situation on the school playground in which a group of kids gangs up on someone and teases and ridicules him or her until someone comes to the rescue.

- Role-play a situation in which a principal becomes involved in a conflict concerning a student being teased at school.

- Role-play a situation in which a student who has been constantly teased and tormented brings a gun or knife to school and threatens to get even.

In the Spotlight

To recognize the uniqueness of each student in your class, a name will be drawn each week and a student will be picked to be "in the spotlight." When it is your turn to be "in the spotlight," you will get special privileges, such as being first to go out for recess, and you will also have an opportunity to tell your classmates about yourself. This is your moment to "shine" and to give others a chance to see what makes you special.

A table and bulletin board will be set up in the classroom just for you. During your spotlight week, bring pictures of you and your family to post on the bulletin board. You can also display items that tell about you and what makes you special—souvenirs from trips and vacations, samples of your hobbies and collections, and other meaningful items. You are responsible for putting up the display at the beginning of the week and taking it down on Friday so the table and bulletin board are ready for the next classmate, whose name is drawn to be in the spotlight the following week. If you have a valuable collection such as baseball cards, coins, etc., don't bring it to school. Your teacher can't be responsible for valuable items, and you certainly don't want anything to happen to them. Bring in photographs of your collection instead.

At the end of the week, when it is time to tell about yourself, you can either have a classmate interview you and ask you questions about your life, or you can just talk about yourself. Plan on a 15-minute presentation. Allow time at the conclusion of your presentation to answer questions from your classmates.

Here are some ideas for things you might want to share when you are "in the spotlight":

- the best day of your life
- the worst day of your life
- the funniest thing that ever happened to you
- things you enjoy doing after school
- pets you have
- the greatest place you ever visited
- a problem or difficulty you have overcome
- a prize or other recognition you have earned
- things you are interested in

Celebrations

Learning about the customs and celebrations of other cultures is a good way to build understanding among groups of people. For this exercise, your teacher will divide your class into teams of five or six students. Each group will choose one of the holidays listed below or another holiday approved by your teacher. Team members will do research to learn how and where the holiday originated, why it is important, and how it is celebrated. Find out about the foods that are eaten on your holiday, songs that are sung, dances that are performed, and other unique features of the celebration. With your team, prepare a skit that will teach others about the holiday you have chosen.

Suggestions:

- Kwanzaa
- Purim
- Sukkos
- Bastille Day
- Tet
- Chinese New Year
- Chinese Lantern Festival
- Kuomboka
- Odwira

- Urini Nal
- Powwow
- Diwali
- Holi
- Cinco de Mayo
- El Día de Los Muertos
- Presidents' Day
- Martin Luther King, Jr., Day

Write a Skit

Write or create a skit portraying someone your age showing intolerance to others through rude or cruel behavior. You may use one of the following situations, or make up your own:

- at a game during recess on the school playground
- in the school cafeteria
- in the classroom while working on a class project
- on the school bus
- on a school field trip
- during a disagreement with a teacher or aide
- with a substitute teacher
- with a parent
- with a brother or sister
- with a classmate who has a learning disability
- with a classmate who has a physical disability

Ask classmates to play the parts of roles you create. In your skit, show the actions that lead to the confrontation or problem. Write the script in such a way that each person involved gets to express what he or she is thinking and feeling. Then show a way (or ways) the situation might be peacefully resolved. Use simple props to get your message across. Lead the class in a discussion at the conclusion of your skit.

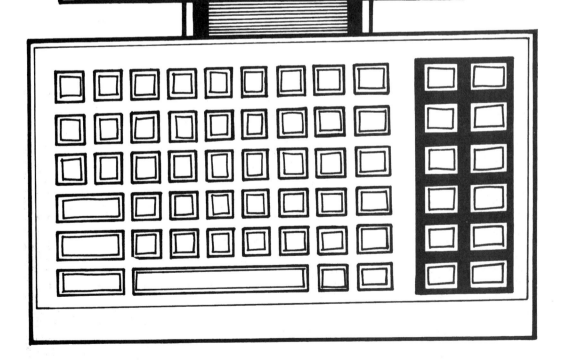

Research
and
Writing Projects

First Impressions

On a separate piece of paper, write a story about a time you formed a hasty opinion of someone before you got to know him or her. In your story, answer some or all of the following questions:

- When did you first meet this person?

- How did you meet?

- What was your first impression of this person?

- How did you get to know him or her better?

- What things did you discover you have in common?

- In what ways are you different?

- What is your relationship like today?

- What did you learn from this experience?

- How has this experience changed the way you form opinions about and treat people you have just met?

Remember to:

- think of a good title

- indent each paragraph

- proofread for spelling, grammar, and punctuation

Wish Poem

Write a wish poem on the topic of tolerance. The wish poem has five lines and follows this structure:

line 1 — is the opening statement, *"I wish I could . . ."*
line 2 — tells how you would start
line 3 — lists three words that end in "ing"
line 4 — starts with the word *always*
line 5 — is a single word—an adverb

Example:

I wish I could stop all the hate in the world
I'd start being more tolerant of others myself—
Helping, sharing, listening,
Always trying to understand the other person's side,
Compassionately.

Contrast Poem

A contrast poem shows two different sides or aspects of a topic or theme.

Write a contrast poem about tolerance. In the first part of your poem, show examples of intolerance. In the second part, show positive aspects of tolerance. Your contrast poem does not have to rhyme. However, each part, or stanza, should have the same number of lines.

Example:

Name calling,
Hurting people's feelings,
Judging people by the color of their skin,
Being impatient with people who have learning or physical disabilities,
Stereotyping people—
Thinking only your way is right.

Listening and respecting the opinions of others,
Treating people as individuals—
Taking the time to know what a person is truly like,
Learning to compromise.
Putting yourself in the other person's shoes,
Being patient and understanding.

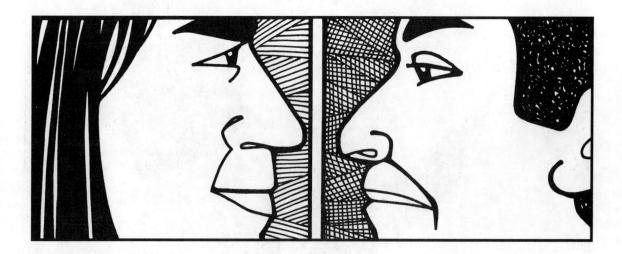

A Poem About Tolerance

On a separate piece of paper, write a poem about tolerance. If you have trouble getting started, try answering some or all of the questions below. They can be answered in any order, and you can add other ideas of your own as you go.

- Where is tolerance born?
- What color is tolerance?
- What does tolerance look like?
- What does tolerance sound like?
- What does tolerance taste like?
- What does tolerance feel like?
- If you could give tolerance to someone, to whom would you give it?

Example

Tolerance is born from kindness, patience, and accepting others for who they really are,

Tolerance is the palest shade of yellow—peaceful, mellow, and calm—never angry like red or impatient like purple,

Slow-motion waves rolling gently upon the beach remind me of tolerance,

Tolerance is a whisper, a soft breeze, a feather spiraling in circles from the sky,

Tolerance tastes like cotton candy and snowflakes melting on my tongue,

Tolerance feels like a warm blanket on a cold winter night,

How I would love to wrap tolerance in a package tied with multicolored ribbons and leave it on the doorsteps of those filled with prejudice and hate.

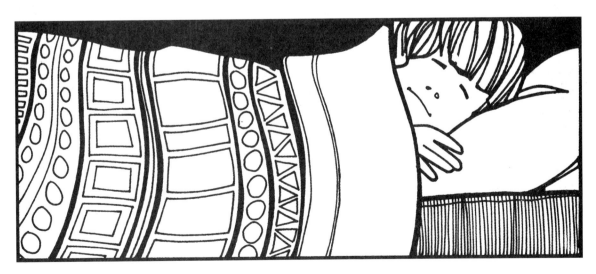

Secret Pals

Your teacher will put the names of all the students in your class in a box. Each of you will pick a name, and this person will become your secret pal for two weeks. As the title of this project implies, the name of your secret pal should be kept secret! It is important not to reveal the name of your secret pal to anyone. If you start telling your best friends the name of your secret pal, word will probably get back to him or her. It's a lot more fun to keep your secret pal guessing who you are.

There will be many opportunities to do thoughtful things for your secret pal during the two weeks, such as:

- sending a card for a special occasion such as a birthday or holiday

- leaving notes on his or her desk

- sending jokes, letters, or cards

- leaving a treat on his or her desk

If your secret pal turns out to be someone who is a close friend who might recognize your handwriting, be sure to disguise your writing on any cards or notes you send.

Under your teacher's supervision, plan a secret pal party to be held at the end of the two weeks. Think of a game or other creative ways that the identities of all the secret pals might be revealed.

People Who Count

On a separate sheet of paper, make a list of the following:

- the names of the two wealthiest women in the United States
- the names of the two wealthiest men in the United States
- the names of three people who have won the Pulitzer Prize
- the names of three people who have won the Nobel Prize
- the names of the women and men who won the Oscar™ at the Academy Awards for best actress and best actor for the last three years
- the names of the last five teams who won the World Series
- the names of the people who won the Heisman Trophy for the last two years

The people above are tops in their fields. But most people can't remember their names.

Now make a separate list of the following:

- the names of two teachers who took a personal interest in you and helped you in school
- the names of three friends who supported you and were there when you really needed them
- the names of two people with whom you enjoy talking and spending time
- the names of two people who treated you with kindness and compassion
- the names of two people who made you feel special and unique

Remember—the people who have the greatest impact on your life may not be those who have the most money or the most awards and trophies. The people who make a difference in your life are the ones who show they care about *you!*

Empathy Exercise

To the Teacher:

Read the following instructions to the class. Pause after each step, giving students time to make choices and share their feelings.

1. Make a list of 10 things that are most special and important to you. These may be people, objects, abilities, places, or anything that comes to mind. You may need to combine or divide some things in order to come up with 10. For example, you could divide your family into my mom, my dad, my brother, my sister, etc., or just refer to your whole extended family as "relatives."

2. When your list of 10 items is complete, read it slowly to yourself. Think about how you feel about the list.

3. Now cross off one thing on your list. Draw a line through it. How do you feel?

4. Cross off something else. It doesn't matter which one—just cross it off.

5. Now cross off two more things. How do you feel now?

6. Look at your list and the things that are left. Cross off one more thing.

7. Now cross off the first thing on your list. How do you feel?

8. There are now four things left on your list. Cross off two of them.

9. Draw a line through one of the two things that are left. How do you feel?

10. Now draw a line through the last thing on your list. How do you feel?

Many of the elderly people living in nursing homes, sitting on park benches, passing you on the sidewalk have "crossed off everything on their lists." They have lost their homes, families, friends, mobility, and independence. They have lost everything they cared about. They go through every day feeling what you are feeling right now. Only their "lists" and their losses are real!

This empathy exercise may help you "see" and understand elderly people better. Write a brief essay describing how this exercise affected you and your outlook towards the elderly.

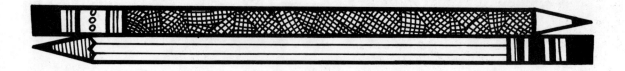

To the Rescue

Write a short story about a young person and his or her family who lose everything in a natural disaster such as a hurricane, a tornado, a fire, a flood, or an earthquake. Imagine that this person's home and family possessions have been destroyed. In your story, describe the ways neighbors and friends show compassion. Try to capture the feelings of the family as people offer help and support. You may decide to put yourself in the story as one of the victims, or as a relative, neighbor, friend, or rescue worker.

Taking Steps Towards Tolerance and Compassion
© The Learning Works, Inc.

Letter to a Newspaper

In your local newspaper, find and read articles dealing with tolerance, as well as ones that reflect intolerance. Write a letter to your local newspaper and express your views on one of these articles. Offer suggestions on ways to improve or address the situation.

You can also choose to write about tolerance at your school and give positive examples of ways in which students go out of their way to help their classmates and to show compassion for each other.

Check your letter to make sure your ideas are clear and that the spelling and punctuation are correct. Be sure to sign the letter, and include the name of your school and your age.

Send your letter to the editor of the newspaper. You can usually find the editor's name and the address of the newspaper on the page that features letters to the editor.

A Recipe for Tolerance

Imagine a world at peace where everyone gets along with his or her neighbors, where nations exist side by side without fighting, where no person is the object of hate, discrimination, or prejudice.

On a separate piece of white paper, create a recipe card like the one below. Write an original recipe for tolerance. Include the following items on your recipe card:

• the name of your recipe

• the ingredients and quantities needed

• the directions for assembling the recipe

• cooking instructions

• the number the recipe serves

Illustrate your recipe card.

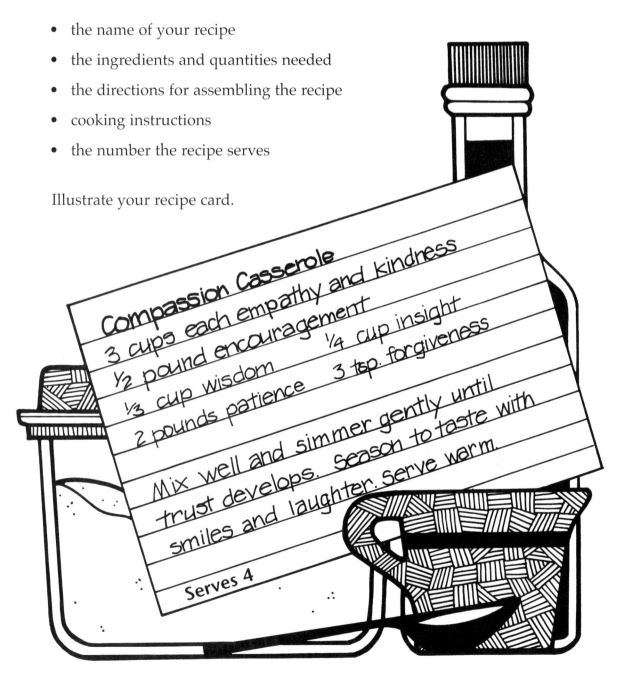

Compassion Casserole
3 cups each empathy and kindness
½ pound encouragement   ¼ cup insight
⅓ cup wisdom   3 tsp. forgiveness
2 pounds patience
Mix well and simmer gently until trust develops. Season to taste with smiles and laughter. Serve warm.
Serves 4

Remember When

Think about a time when you acted in a rude and selfish way with someone else—a family member, a close friend, a classmate, a relative, a neighbor, or a stranger. What happened? What did you do? How did you feel about yourself?

Now think about a time you were helpful or polite to a person with whom you previously felt unfriendly or uncomfortable. What were the circumstances, and what happened? How did you feel about yourself?

On a separate piece of paper, write about both incidents.

You can also divide a piece of white art paper in half. Draw a picture of what you did. Write a sentence or two explaining your actions.

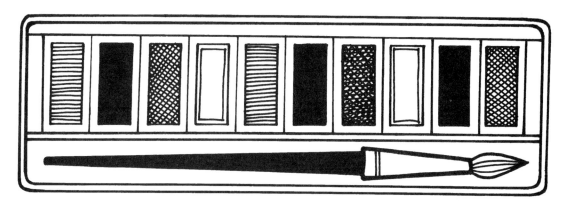

Art Projects

Tiles for Tolerance

What does the word *tolerance* mean to you? Capture the spirit and meaning of the word through an original painting done on a ceramic tile. You will need a tile and enamel paint in various colors.

First, sketch several designs on scratch paper. Then select your favorite, and draw it on the tile with pencil. Finish your design by painting it with enamel. Here are some fun things you can do with your finished tile:

- Hang it on your bedroom wall.

- Use the tile as a hot plate.

- Present your tile to someone as a special gift.

- Add your tolerance tile to the tiles made by your classmates and, with your teacher's help, make a border going around a classroom bulletin board. You can also make a collage using all the tiles for a display in your classroom or school office. What a great way to greet visitors!

Sample Tiles

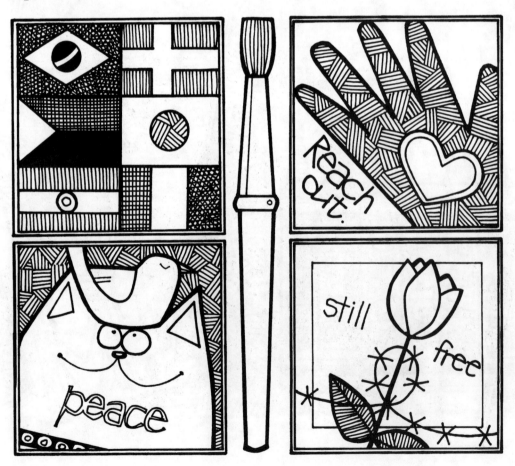

A Photo Essay

There is a popular saying that a picture is worth a thousand words. Look at the world of tolerance and compassion through the lens of a camera, and create a photo essay of people demonstrating kindness, understanding, and tolerance towards others. Take pictures at school and in your neighborhood that show people being tolerant and compassionate towards others. Here are some examples of scenes you might photograph:

- kids playing cooperatively on the school playground

- students sharing art supplies while working on a project

- kids waiting patiently in line in the cafeteria

- a student tutoring or helping a classmate

- a child holding a door open at a store for a person who is in a wheelchair

When your pictures have been developed, mount them on poster board. Add words and phrases cut out from the headlines of magazines to capture the spirit of tolerance and compassion. Display your poster for your classmates to enjoy.

People of Tolerance Hall of Fame

Select a famous person of tolerance and learn more about him or her. Take notes as you do your research, and then prepare an oral presentation about the person you selected. Here are some suggestions for topics to cover in your oral presentation:

- How would you describe this person's childhood?

- What events in his or her life helped shape the person he or she became?

- What fascinating facts did you learn about this person?

- What difficulties did he or she have to overcome?

- What events in this person's life helped him or her become more tolerant of other people?

- If you could interview this person, what three questions would you ask him or her?

- In what ways did this person of tolerance influence the world?

- If you had to choose a person living today who was most like the person you selected for your research, who would it be and why? In what ways are they similar? In what ways are they different?

When presenting your report, you may dress in character and pretend you are the person on whom you are reporting. Your report would then be given in the "first person." For example, if you were presenting your report on Martin Luther King, Jr., you might begin your oral presentation as follows:

"My name is Martin Luther King, Jr. I was a famous civil rights leader who cared deeply about treating everyone with tolerance and kindness."

Design a Postage Stamp

Pretend that you have been commissioned by the United States Postal Service to design a postage stamp to promote tolerance. Your design should convey the message of treating people with respect. Try several designs and ideas on scratch paper. Then select your favorite design, and draw it on white art paper. Use felt markers, crayons, or colored pencils to color your design. Be sure to include the price of your stamp.

Taking Steps Towards Tolerance and Compassion
© The Learning Works, Inc.

Compassion Quilt

Brainstorm words and thoughts that you associate with the word *compassion*. You can also use personal thoughts or quotations from famous people. Here are some examples of words or phrases you could use:

- helping others

- patience

- understanding for those less fortunate

- empathy

Construct a compassion quilt using shapes cut from wallpaper samples or colored construction paper. On each shape, write one of your words, phrases, thoughts, or quotations about compassion. Glue the shapes together as shown below.

You cannot do a kindness too soon, for you never know how soon it will be too late.

—*Ralph Waldo Emerson*

The "You Are Special" Box

This project is a great way to get you thinking about what makes each of your classmates special. Your teacher will ask each of you to bring a medium-sized box, such as a shoe box, a tissue box, or a clean 10-inch pizza box from home.

Cover your box with colored paper, and cut a hole in it for receiving mail. Write your name on the outside of the box. You can decorate the box if you like. Your teacher will find a place to display all of the boxes.

Over a period of one month, you will be asked to fill out "You Are Special" slips to place in the boxes of all your classmates. Your comments should focus on something special about the person:

- something nice this person did
- what makes this person a good friend
- a way you've seen this classmate improve
- a characteristic you like, such as his or her sense of humor

You will also be given a class list so you can mark off classmates' names as you put "You Are Special" slips in their boxes. Of course, it's easy to write something positive about the kids you know well. But this exercise is designed to make you stop and think about classmates who aren't among your close friends. Find something positive to say about each student even if you don't know him or her very well. Just be sure your comments are honest and sincere.

Don't peek at your notes as you get them! Wait until the end of the month, when your box will be filled with comments from classmates telling why you are special. Then open the box and enjoy reading your mail!

A Wall of Compassion

Work with your classmates to create a wall of compassion in your classroom.

Your teacher will tape a long sheet of white butcher paper to a classroom wall. Before drawing on the mural, brainstorm ideas for different aspects of compassion you can portray through your art. For example, you might want to show people planting a tree to beautify a community, a person helping someone who is in a wheelchair, or a group of kids holding a car wash as a fund-raiser for a worthy cause. After your list is complete, vote on those the majority feel should be included in the mural.

Make a small-scale drawing of the mural, sketching pictures of the scenes the class has chosen and fitting them together. Then enlarge the drawing onto the butcher paper (as shown below) or use an overhead projector. Use pencil so that changes can be made if necessary.

Use paint, crayons, and / or markers to color the mural. Have everyone sign their work. Exhibit your completed mural where many people will see and enjoy it!

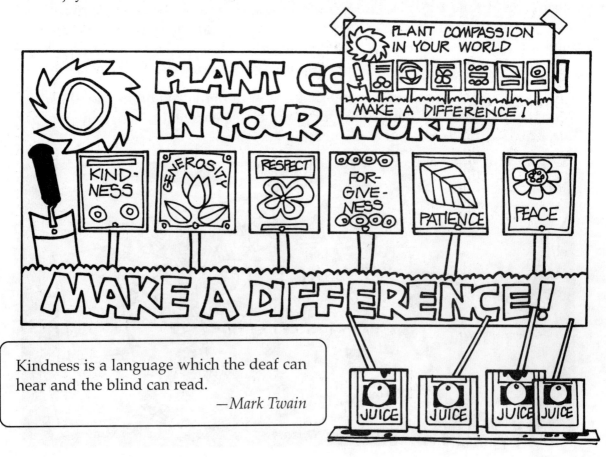

Kindness is a language which the deaf can hear and the blind can read.
— *Mark Twain*

A Step in the Right Direction

Think about a step you could take to make a difference in the world. It could be donating clothes you no longer wear to a homeless shelter, serving food at a soup kitchen, or volunteering to help a senior citizen with a chore. Your idea could be something you have actually done to help others or something you can see yourself doing in the future. Then follow these simple steps:

1. Use a pencil to trace around your bare foot or around your shoe on a sheet of white art paper.

2. Inside the image of your foot or shoe, draw pictures or use magazine pictures to illustrate your idea. Add cut-out words and phrases from old magazines to add interest to your work.

3. Cut out your foot or shoe shape and display it on a bulletin board in the classroom along with those of your classmates.

Variation: Lend a Helping Hand

Think about ways you could lend a helping hand to show compassion to others. Then, instead of using your foot or shoe as a pattern, trace around your hand on a sheet of white art paper. Fill the inside of your hand pattern with a drawing of your idea. Cut words from old magazines to paste on your picture.

A Trio of Projects

Design a Poster

Design a poster that teaches other students about tolerance. Use words, pictures, and/or drawings to convey your message. Plan your design on scratch paper, then do the final version on poster board using paint, ink, crayons, colored pencils, or marking pens. Display your poster for others to see.

Design a Bumper Sticker

Design an original bumper sticker that sends a message about tolerance and/or compassion, as shown below.

Create a Tolerance Scrapbook

In your local newspaper, find and read articles dealing with tolerance. Try to find articles that show both tolerance and intolerance towards others. Cut out these articles, and mount them in a scrapbook. Decorate the cover of the scrapbook.

Steps to Take
Towards Tolerance
and Compassion

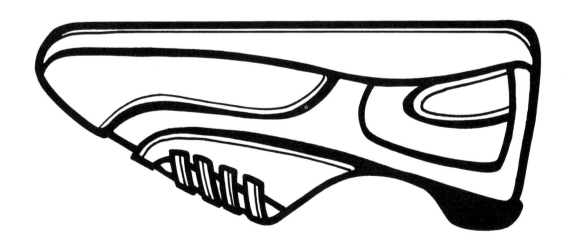

Serve Food at a Shelter

A community shelter is a place where people in need can stay until they get back on their feet. The shelter provides families with a place to spend the night and a place to get healthy meals.

Volunteer with your family to help at a community shelter. Perhaps you can help serve meals and clean up afterwards. Call the shelter first and ask if there are children at the shelter. If there are, you might want to bring along your favorite book to read to them or a game to play together.

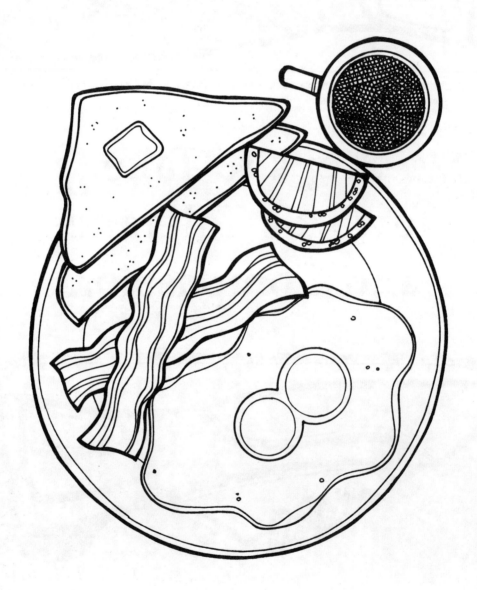

Appreciation Day

> **To the Teacher**
>
> Divide your class into teams of four or five students. Each team will pick someone who works at your school to honor on a day you designate as "Appreciation Day."

You and the members of your team will select a person who works at your school to recognize for the things he or she does to make your school a better place. Here are some suggestions of people you could choose to honor on Appreciation Day:

- art teacher
- cafeteria worker
- classroom aide
- custodian
- music teacher
- noon aide
- office worker

- playground supervisor
- principal
- school crossing guard
- school librarian
- school nurse
- school secretary
- vice-principal

Once you've selected the person you want to recognize, submit his or her name to your teacher. (Your teacher will make sure there are no duplications.)

As a group, brainstorm things you could do on Appreciation Day for your special person. Here are some ideas to get your started:

- Bake a batch of cookies.
- Write a group thank-you note.
- Design a giant thank-you card that all members of your group can sign.
- Write a letter to the editor of your local newspaper telling about this person's contributions.
- Make a banner on the computer.

Variation:

Plan an Appreciation Day for someone in your community such as a firefighter, a librarian, a police officer—or anyone else who makes your neighborhood a better place in which to live.

Toys, Games, and Sports Equipment Roundup

This is a great project that your whole class can work on together to help kids who have less than you. Your teacher will designate one week as "Toys, Games, and Sports Equipment Roundup Week." Several students will be asked to bring in large, empty boxes for the collection. Here's what you will do:

- Look at home for toys, board games, and puzzles you have outgrown or no longer play with. They don't have to be in perfect condition, but they should not be missing any pieces. Toys should not have any broken parts that might make them unsafe.

- Also go through your closets at home and look for old baseball bats, footballs, skateboards, catcher's mitts, tennis rackets, volleyballs, jump ropes, and other sports equipment you don't use.

- Be sure to ask your mom or dad for permission to donate these things before taking them to school.

- Check with your friends, relatives, and neighbors to see if they have any of these items to donate during the week of your roundup.

Donate the items to children at a homeless shelter, to a childcare center, to a church, synagogue, or mosque, or to needy families with children.

Disaster Aid

You can demonstrate compassion towards others by lending a helping hand following a natural disaster such as a hurricane, tornado, flood, or fire.

Here are some projects you and your classmates or family can do to help people who have lost their possessions, been injured, or had damage to their homes. (Be sure to find out first what is needed.)

- Donate household supplies, clothing, food, and toys.

- Collect and distribute blankets.

- Help with clean-up operations (under adult supervision) once the area has been declared safe.

- Raise money to help a family in your community.

- Make and put up posters for lost pets.

- Make sandwiches and serve them to rescue workers and volunteers.

Read-a-Thon Fundraiser

"Activate" your compassion by earning money for people in need. Holding a Read-a-Thon is a fun way to help others while sharpening your reading skills and enjoying some great books.

Participate in a class Read-a-Thon by seeing how many books you can read in a specified period of time, such as a month. As a class, everyone will vote on a charitable organization in the community to be the recipient of the money that is collected.

Before beginning, ask your family, friends, relatives, and neighbors to sign up as sponsors. Each sponsor pledges a set amount of money for each book you read during the Read-a-Thon month. Let your sponsors know that the money they pledge is going to a charitable organization.

Get your teacher's approval before starting each book to be sure you are reading a book that is suitable for your reading ability. Your teacher will give you a form to fill out as you finish each book. At the end of the Read-a-Thon month, collect the pledges from your sponsors. (Checks should be made payable to the organization the class selected.)

To the Teacher:

- Make a Read-a-Thon sign-up form similar to the one on page 73 for each student.

- Ribbons or bookmarks can be presented to your students who participate in the Read-a-Thon. Solicit gift certificates from local bookstores to give to students who read a specific number of books or who raise the most money through pledges.

- Plan a special ceremony when it is time to present the checks to the organization your class selected. Invite a reporter from your local newspaper to cover the story.

Read-a-Thon Fundraiser
(continued)

Check the front pages of your telephone directory to find the names of organizations that serve children in your community. Here are some ideas to get you started:

- Big Brothers/Big Sisters of America
- an after-school program
- a shelter for the homeless
- the pediatric wing of a hospital
- the Special Olympics
- March of Dimes
- Leukemia Society
- Juvenile Diabetes Foundation
- Save the Children
- Boys' and Girls' Clubs of America
- Camp Fire Boys and Girls
- Cystic Fibrosis Foundation
- Girl Scouts of the U.S.A.
- Boy Scouts of America
- U.S. Committee for UNICEF
- National Association for the Deaf

Send each of your sponsors a thank-you note for his or her donation and support of the Read-a-Thon program.

Sample

Read-a-Thon Sign Up Sheet

My name _____

The money I raise will be donated to _____

I plan to read _____ books. (Use the back of this form if you need more room.)

book title	date completed
_____	_____
_____	_____
_____	_____
_____	_____

sponsor's name, address, and telephone	amount pledged per book	total amount pledged
_____	_____	_____
_____	_____	_____
_____	_____	_____
_____	_____	_____

Taking Steps Towards Tolerance and Compassion
© The Learning Works, Inc.

Gift Baskets for Senior Citizens

There are many senior citizens living alone in convalescent homes and retirement communities without any friends or family to visit them. Show you care by making a gift basket for a senior citizen for a holiday such as Valentine's Day, Thanksgiving, Christmas, or Hanukkah. Your gift basket can also be related to the special interests of your senior friend.

Inexpensive baskets can often be found at thrift stores and rummage sales. Before filling your basket, ask the facility staff what items are most needed or would be most appreciated. Here are some examples of baskets you can create:

a bath basket filled with
- scented soaps
- a bath sponge
- bubble bath
- a wash cloth
- dusting powder

a snack basket filled with
- cheese
- crackers
- fruit
- hard candies

(Check with the facility staff to be sure the recipient doesn't have any dietary restrictions.)

a book lover's basket filled with
- large print books
- magazines
- a bookmark made by you

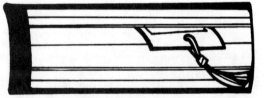

a gardener's basket filled with
- gardening gloves
- potting soil
- a flower pot
- seeds to plant
- small gardening tools

a letter writer's basket filled with
- note cards
- stationery
- postage stamps
- envelopes
- a pen

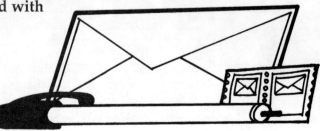

Compassion for Animals

If you have ever adopted a furry, friendly pet at an animal shelter, you probably have a great appreciation for the job that these organizations do. Many communities have facilities that provide care for animals that are lost, abused, or unwanted. With your class or family, visit one of these shelters and learn more about the work that is done there. Services offered by animal shelters vary widely. Some shelters deal only with pets; others handle livestock and/or wildlife. They may offer educational programs or wildlife clinics.

Volunteering to work at an animal shelter is a great way to show your compassion for animals. Ask the shelter staff about the opportunities that are available for junior volunteers.

Many zoos also have student volunteer programs. If there is a zoo in your community, find out how you can participate in such a program. If there isn't a zoo, find out if a nature center, an aquarium, or a wildlife refuge could use your help.

Compassion applies to pets as well as people. Pets need to be treated with kindness, patience, and love. A compassionate person would never hurt or mistreat an animal. Here are some things you can do to show compassion for pets.

- Make sure your pet is properly groomed and taken to the vet for regular checkups.

- Take time to play with your dog or cat—even when you are busy.

- Walk your dog often so he or she gets plenty of exercise.

- Volunteer to walk a neighbor's dog, especially if the dog lives with a disabled person who can't get out easily.

- If you see a dog wandering loose, report it to a parent or teacher so that the animal isn't injured.

- Talk to your mom or dad about spaying or neutering your pet.

Taking Steps Towards Tolerance and Compassion
© The Learning Works, Inc.

Pet Presents You Can Make

Share kindness with pets by making them toys to play with. Here are some creative presents you can make for pets at the Humane Society shelter, classroom pets, pets belonging to your friends and neighbors, or your own critters. (Be sure to use nontoxic paints.)

- Decorate a paper bag in which a cat, rabbit, or guinea pig can play.

- Tie a tennis ball inside an old sock for tossing and tugging games with a dog.

- Make a rattle for a pet rabbit by taping a few buttons or pebbles inside a small juice can that you decorate.

Heidi's House

- Create a cat clubhouse from an old carton. Cut windows and doors, and add decorations.

- Plant birdseed or grass in an empty margarine tub, and let your parakeet or cat nibble the greens.

A Story of Compassion: Jason Young

After arson destroyed the Friendship Missionary Baptist Church in Millen, Georgia, a group of 40 volunteers from Congregation B'nai B'rith and the First United Methodist Church in Santa Barbara, California, traveled to Georgia to rebuild the wooden structure.

Among the volunteers was a 13-year-old boy named Jason Young, an eighth-grader at Laguna Blanca School. Jason, accompanied by his father, Jeff, and his brother, Jared, worked with the other volunteers in sweltering 100-degree weather to rebuild the church. The volunteers did the electrical work, insulation, dry walling, plumbing, and landscaping for the new church. Jason helped lay the cement and bricks for the project.

This was the second church-building project for Jason. In 1999, Jason went with his dad and brother to help rebuild a burned African-American church in South Carolina.

When Jason celebrated his Bar Mitzvah, a ceremony in the Jewish religion in which a young man marks his entrance into manhood and is called to read from the Torah, he was asked to take on more responsibility and to do *mitzvot*—kind deeds—for others.

Jason decided to take the $900 he had received for his Bar Mitzvah and donate the money to construct a wheelchair access ramp for the new church. The church did not have the funds to build such a ramp, so Jason came to the rescue. With the money he donated, a new ramp was constructed that gave members who were confined to wheelchairs an opportunity to have better access to church services and activities.

The ramp was built to meet the standards of the Americans with Disabilities Act. It had to be a certain width, have a specific grade of slope, and have a landing to accommodate the wheelchairs of the church members. Jason actually worked with the group to help build the ramp.

The congregants treated the volunteers to a dinner and snacks as they worked on the project. The volunteer group was praised for completing the task—a project that normally would have taken months—in only a week.

Jason was honored in a special ramp dedication ceremony in Millen, complete with a ribbon-cutting ceremony. Church services were held where people of different races, religions, and beliefs came together to worship under one roof. An act filled with hatred and prejudice was transformed into a project that brought people together to help each other in compassion and concern. Jason deserves a lot of credit for his unselfish donation and outstanding example of compassion.

Taking Steps Towards Tolerance and Compassion
© The Learning Works, Inc.

Share Your Story

There are many young people like Jason Young who have taken steps to show tolerance and compassion towards others. We would like to hear about something special that you did for someone that reflects your tolerance or compassion.

Before submitting your story, check with your dad or mom and get his or her permission. Send us your story following these simple rules:

1. Use a computer or typewriter when writing the final draft of your story. Handwritten copies cannot be accepted.

2. Your story must not be more than two pages long. Here are some questions you might want to answer in your story:

   • When and where did the incident take place?

   • What events led up to the action you took?

   • What other people were involved?

   • What did you actually do?

   • How were other people affected?

   • How did you feel about yourself?

   • What did you learn from the experience?

3. Include your name, address, grade level, and the name of your school, so that we can get in touch with you if your story is selected for a future publication. (Stories will not be returned.)

4. Send your stories to:

   The Learning Works, Inc.
   Tolerance and Compassion Stories
   P. O. Box 2723
   Huntington Beach, CA 92647

   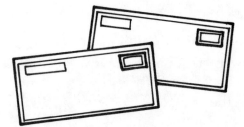

We hope you have enjoyed the activities in this book. We would like to see pictures of projects you made, read copies of poems or essays you wrote about tolerance and compassion, and receive letters from you telling us what you thought about the book.

Send your letters to the address above.

Ideas for a Schoolwide
Tolerance and Compassion Program

To the Teacher:

- Designate tolerance and compassion as themes for one month of the school year. During this month, plan special programs to reinforce the importance of treating each other with respect and kindness. Invite guest speakers from your community to talk at assemblies. Here are some suggestions for people you can invite:

  - a police officer
  - a peace mediator
  - a guidance counselor

- Grow a garden of tolerance and compassion at your school. Have your students fill out flowers and leaves using the patterns on page 80 to acknowledge their acts of tolerance and kindness towards others. Display the flowers on a bulletin board in the school office or cafeteria. Add a white picket fence made from construction paper to the garden.

- Ask the school librarian to make a special display of biographies of people who are known for their compassion towards others. Encourage students to read the life stories of these famous people.

- In the upper grades, teach students about the Holocaust. Invite a survivor from your community to talk to students and answer questions about the Holocaust. Check with a rabbi from your neighborhood synagogue for the names of survivors willing to speak to students.

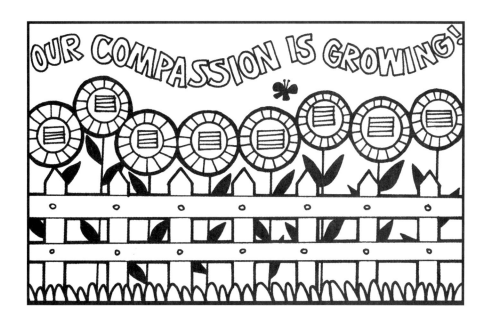

Leaf and Flower Patterns for a
Tolerance and Compassion Garden

To the Teacher: Reproduce these patterns on colored paper and cut them out. After your students have filled in the information, use the flowers to create a tolerance and compassion garden on your bulletin board.

To the Student: On the flower pattern, write a brief description of something you have done for another person that shows tolerance or compassion. Write your name on the leaf.

Patterns

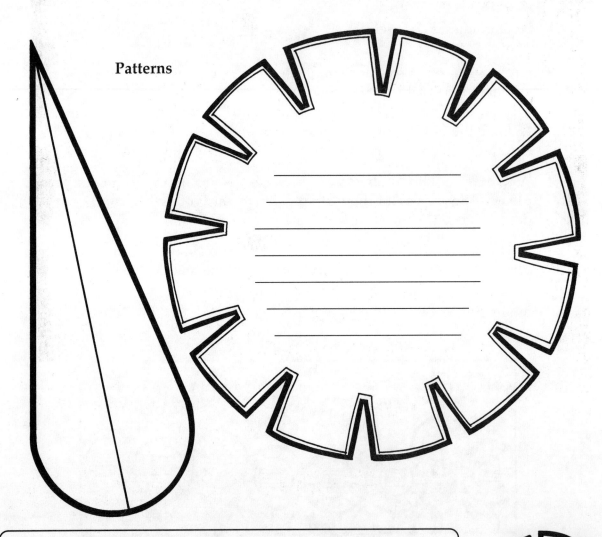

I expect to pass through life but once. If, therefore, there be any kindness I can show, or any good thing I can do to any fellow being, let me do it now, and not defer or neglect it, as I shall not pass this way again.

—*William Penn*